'Kevin DeYoung engagingly explains what the conscience is, how to have a clear one, and why it matters.'

**Andy Naselli**, assistant professor of New Testament and theology at Bethlehem College & Seminary

'Kevin convincingly helps readers to understand how our consciences are intrinsically connected to our spiritual decline or flourishing. As a biblical counselor I am grateful for this resource as it is sure to be helpful for anyone who reads it.'

**Eliza Huie**, author and counselor

'A simple, clear and much-needed focus on an essential element of Christian growth.'

**Jonathan Lamb**, Minister-at-large for Keswick Ministries, Vice-President of IFES

'This is a wonderfully clear teaching about a joyfully clear conscience. It's instructive and even perhaps surprising to hear all the Bible has to say on this topic we too often neglect.'

**Kathleen Nielson**, The Gospel Coalition

'There have not been many modern books written on the place of conscience in the Christian life. I am thrilled that Kevin has written one. Faithfulness to the Bible and clarity of expression are hallmarks of his books. This little book is no exception. I found it stimulating and helpful.'

**Justin Mote**, Director of Training for
The North West Gospel Partnership

'Short enough to read in one sitting, significant enough to change your whole life.'

**Nancy Guthrie**, Bible Teacher and author

'This excellent short book takes us, through the lens of a proper Biblical understanding of conscience, to the heart of the Gospel. It is written for Christians, and will do us much good, but I will feel confident in handing it to those exploring the Christian faith.'

**William Taylor**, St Helen's Bishopsgate, London

# THE ART OF
# TURNING

## FROM SIN TO CHRIST FOR A
## JOYFULLY CLEAR CONSCIENCE

# KEVIN DeYOUNG

10 Publishing
a division of 10ofthose.com

Copyright © 2017 by Kevin DeYoung

First published in Great Britain in 2017

British Library Cataloguing in Publication Data
A record for this book is available from the British Library

ISBN: 978-1-911272-21-2

Designed and typeset by Pete Barnsley (CreativeHoot)

Printed in Denmark by Nørhaven

10Publishing, a division of 10ofthose.com
Unit C, Tomlinson Road, Leyland, PR25 2DY, England

Email: info@10ofthose.com
Website: www.10ofthose.com

# CONTENTS

# 1

# LUTHER'S CONSCIENTIOUS STAND

When Martin Luther rode into the town of Worms in 1521, he was not a confident man.

Luther had long protested against the corruption of the Roman Catholic Church— most famously in 1517 with the posting of his Ninety-five Theses on the door of the Castle Church in Wittenberg. After years of ensuing controversy, Pope Leo X finally excommunicated the German reformer in January 1521. In April of that year, Luther was summoned to appear before the Imperial Diet (Assembly) at Worms to defend his controversial beliefs before the Holy Roman Emperor Charles V. We may think of Luther as big and brash and full of swagger, but he came into Worms so intimidated that on the first day of his defense his statements could barely be understood. The Catholic authorities were threatening to banish him from Charles' empire—a vast territory centered in Germany and spanning central Europe. Luther's livelihood as a professor, and his very life, were at stake.

Luther knew what the authorities wanted him to do: recant his words criticizing the Catholic Church for its teaching and practices. However fearful he may have been at the outset, by the end of the interrogation Luther had gathered his strength. "My conscience is captive to the Word of God," Luther declared. "Thus I cannot and will not repent, for going against my conscience is neither safe nor salutary. I can do no other. Here I stand. God help me. Amen."

On May 26, 1521, the Emperor rendered his decision. Luther was to be placed under a "ban and double ban." This Edict of Worms implored the men and women of the empire:

> . . . *not to take the aforementioned Martin Luther into your houses, not to receive him at*

*court, to give him neither food nor drink, not to hide him, to afford him no help, following, support, or encouragement, either clandestinely or publicly, through words or work. Where you can get him, seize him and empower him, you should capture him and send him to us under tight security.*

Luther was now a man on the run. The powers that be were adamant that Luther and his writings—and anyone sympathetic to his ideas—must be silenced. And yet, Luther was willing to endure all this—expulsion, danger, maybe even death—for the sake of his conscience. In a very real sense, you could say that the history of the Reformation, the history of Europe, and the history of the entire world was, in God's providence, altered because one man refused to violate his conscience.

Praise God Luther took his conscience seriously.

I wonder if you and I are quite so careful with ours.

# 2

# PAUL'S CONSCIENTIOUS DEFENSE

Of course, Martin Luther was not the first, or the most famous, preacher to appeal to his conscience. "For our boast is this," wrote the Apostle Paul, "the testimony of our conscience, that we behaved in the world with simplicity and godly sincerity, not by earthly wisdom but by the grace of God, and supremely so toward you" (2 Cor. 1:12).

Paul's opponents in Corinth thought he was a weak and hypocritical phony. He was (they thought) bold in his letters, but unimpressive in person (2 Cor. 10:1–2). They also charged him with duplicity, saying one thing but doing another. Listen to Paul's defense:

> *Because I was sure of this, I wanted to come to you first, so that you might have a second experience of grace. I wanted to visit you on my way to Macedonia, and to come back to you from Macedonia and have you send me on my way to Judea. Was I vacillating when I wanted to do this? Do I make my plans according to the flesh, ready to say "Yes, yes" and "No, no" at the same time? (2 Cor. 1:15–17).*

Reading between the lines, we can surmise that Paul had written to them telling them of his plans to visit them. Paul was eager to see the Corinthians and pay them a visit. Yet something happened to change the good vibes and force Paul into Plan B. At the last minute, Paul decided not to come to Corinth, not because he was fickle, but because he loved them. As Paul says in verse 23: "But I call God to witness against me—it was to spare you that I refrained from coming again to Corinth."

You can understand the situation from the point of view of the Christians in Corinth. Paul said he was excited to see them. Then he didn't show up. What gives? They considered the change of plans one more reason they couldn't trust Paul. He was weak, fickle, feeble, and frail.

Paul, for his part, knew that his motives were pure. He was not running from trouble. He was not engaging in doubletalk. The only reason Paul didn't show up was because he considered it wise to avoid "another painful visit" (2 Cor. 2:1). The Corinthians were putting up with false teachers and so-called super-apostles. They were heading in the wrong direction. And if Paul showed up at their doorstep, he would have no choice but to sternly rebuke—in person—the people he loved. He wasn't sure the relationship could handle another face-to-face confrontation. So Paul decided it would be better to put off his planned trip. The letter of 2 Corinthians is a defense of Paul's ministry in response to the lies of these false apostles and the misunderstandings taking root in Corinth.

This brings us back to verse 12 in chapter 1 of the letter. Notice three things Paul mentions in his defense.

## 1. SIMPLICITY

First, he says he has acted "with simplicity." By this he means that his motives were pure, and he really did desire to see the Corinthians. When he said he would visit them, he was not making plans "by earthly wisdom." He was not trying to be calculating. He was not interested in political maneuvering or trickery.

## 2. SINCERITY

Second, Paul says he acted with "godly sincerity." When he decided not to visit, and then explained his reason, Paul was forthright, honest, and candid. He did not tell them one thing, but mean another. He was not trying to be coy or evasive. He meant everything he said to them. His change of plans was motivated solely by a concern for their well-being. As such, the criticisms leveled against him were not fair.

Many of us have faced the same kind of criticisms. Plans change. Sometimes it's the better part of wisdom *not* to follow through on our original intentions. If I so much as mention to my kids that we *might* go to the movies tomorrow, it is perceived as the promise of all promises that has ever been uttered. And yet, as a parent, I know I can't always follow through on every possible plan I dare to mention. But that doesn't stop the kids from loudly protesting: "You never do anything for us! You promised! How could you?!" Paul is facing a similar situation. He wanted to come to Corinth, but it turns out the best thing to do was to wait. Simple as that.

## 3. CONSCIENCE

Third, Paul mentions "the testimony of [his] conscience." In other words, despite a myriad of accusations and allegations, Paul's conscience testifies that he has acted in a God-honoring way.

There are more than a dozen instances in the New Testament where Paul mentions the testimony of his conscience. In Acts 23:1, after being arrested and put in chains before the Jewish council, we read that Paul looked intently at the council and said, "Brothers, I have lived my life before God in all good conscience." In

Romans 9:1 he writes, "I am speaking the truth in Christ—I am not lying; my conscience bears me witness in the Holy Spirit." In 2 Timothy 1:3 he declares, "I thank God whom I serve, as did my ancestors, with a clear conscience." Though probably not written by Paul, Hebrews 13:18 adds: "Pray for us, for we are sure that we have a clear conscience, desiring to act honorably in all things."

It's striking that Paul would "boast" in his conscience. This may seem surprising since Paul elsewhere says we are not to boast except in the Lord (1 Cor. 1:31; 13:4; Gal. 6:14). Paul may be borrowing the language of the super-apostles in an ironic way. These false teachers were happy to boast of their credentials and accomplishments (see 2 Cor. 11:1–15). Paul replies, in effect, "If you want me to boast about something, I'll boast in the testimony of my conscience, that I'm not like any of you!"

Notice, Paul doesn't over-apologize just to get the Corinthians off his back. He doesn't say sorry for something he's not sorry for. He doesn't confess a sin when his conscience says he hasn't sinned. Paul understood what our culture often does not: the fact that you are offended does not mean that I am automatically guilty. Of course, we want to be teachable and humble. We want to be open to correction. But just because someone else is bent out of shape doesn't mean we've dented anything. Ultimately, God is the final judge, and we do not need to grovel for mercy when a good, functioning conscience has not condemned us for doing anything wrong. A clean conscience is a precious thing—for Paul and for us.

# 3

# WHAT EXACTLY IS OUR CONSCIENCE?

As much as the Bible talks about the conscience, it's remarkable how little we hear of it today. It's not something pastors often teach on and not something most believers consider in daily discipleship. And yet, if you read our ancestors in the faith (especially the Puritans), you'll find that they were obsessed with the conscience. In a good way. They paid careful attention to how the conscience works, the role it plays in bringing people to Christ, and how it is indispensable in leading us into holiness.

So what is the conscience? Here's my definition: *the conscience is the moral faculty within human beings that assesses what is good and what is bad.* The Greek word for "conscience" is *suneidesis*. In this compound word, *sun* is the prefix for "with," and *desis* is a form of the word "knowing." Similarly, the Latin word root of our English word could be translated "with knowledge" (*con-scientia*). In other words, the conscience is what aids us in acquiring knowledge—in particular, knowledge and understanding in ethical and moral matters.

There is a close connection between the work of the Holy Spirit and the operation of the conscience. John Flavel, a Puritan clergyman and author, observed that the conscience "is God's spy, and man's overseer." The Spirit convicts us of evil by showing the truth about sin, the truth about Christ, and the truth about his glory (John 16:8–15). When the Holy Spirit shines a light on what is bad (or good) in us, it is then the role of the conscience to appropriate the work of the Spirit (John 3:20–21). This is why Paul can say: "my conscience bears me witness in the Holy Spirit" (Rom. 9:1). The Holy Spirit works in tandem with the conscience to produce in us a life of godliness and peace.

The classic explanation of how the conscience works (or is supposed to work) can be found in Romans 2:14–15: "For when Gentiles, who do not have the law, by nature do what the law requires, they are a law to themselves, even though they do not have the law. They show that the work of the law is written on their hearts, while their conscience also bears witness, and their conflicting thoughts accuse or even excuse them." The conscience acts as both a prosecuting attorney and a defense attorney.

First, then, the conscience is to be a prosecuting attorney to convict us of sin when we violate God's law. The conscience keeps us up at night. It gives us a pit in our stomach. It reminds us of our offenses against God. When working properly, the conscience is that sixth sense which impresses upon us a feeling of guilt for deeds misdone.

But second, on the other hand, the conscience is also to be a defense attorney. We usually think of the conscience as that little voice in our head that tells us that our mom was right or that we are bad to the bone. That can be the work of the conscience, but the conscience should also defend us against false allegations. Notice how Paul said, "their conflicting thoughts accuse or even *excuse*" (my italics). Our conscience helps us to face the accusations of the devil, our enemies, and other slanderers. This is what Paul says, in effect, in 2 Corinthians 1:12: "My conscience is clear. You may be really cross at me for not coming to visit you, but as far as I know in my own head and heart, I have not done anything wrong."

Having a conscience is one mark of being a sentient human being. Scripture sometimes speaks of people "who do not know their right hand from their left" (Jon. 4:11), or of "children, who . . . have no knowledge of good or evil" (Deut. 1:39). Knowing right from wrong is what makes us functioning adults. To have a malfunctioning conscience is to be less than human.

Many of you will know the story of Pinocchio. I remember the story as I learned it from the Disney cartoon version. The wood-carver Geppetto wants his puppet Pinocchio to be a real boy. Once this wish is granted, Jiminy Cricket is assigned to be Pinocchio's conscience.

As a child, I was terrified by the movie, because, of course, Pinocchio doesn't stay a little boy for long. He falls in with the wrong crowd, and his lack of truth-telling gets him into trouble. His nose grows long as a sign that lies eventually become as plain as the nose on your face. As he continues to lie and ignore Jiminy Cricket, Pinocchio starts turning into a donkey. He blurts out a "hee-haw" in the middle of sentences. He starts braying. Donkey ears pop out of his head. A donkey tail sprouts from his backside. The boy is becoming an animal.

There is more going on in this story than we realize as children. The crux of the tale is that as Pinocchio ignores his conscience, he becomes more like a beast. He becomes something less than human. A conscience is not only indispensable to living a life pleasing to God and enjoying peace with God; it is essential for living as the human beings God made us to be.

# 4

# CONSCIENCES THAT MISFIRE

The problem is that this God-given faculty, which is meant to be instructed by the Holy Spirit and shaped by the Word of God, can misfire. The Bible gives us several examples of consciences gone bad.

## 1. AN EVIL CONSCIENCE

According to Hebrews 10:22, we must draw near to God "with a true heart in full assurance of faith, with our hearts sprinkled clean from an *evil conscience* and our bodies washed with pure water" (my italics). The context for this verse is important. We are told to "hold fast" to our confession of faith and to keep doing "good works" as we encourage one another to persevere (vv. 23–25). By implication, then, an evil conscience is one that accuses us of wrongdoing, but the wrongdoing is not dealt with. When that little voice in your head—whether by the light of nature or common grace or by the prompting of the Holy Spirit—keeps convicting you of sin, and yet you keep on doing the thing you know to be sin, that's an evil conscience. It's a conscience that is ignored and not dealt with.

As a boy, my best friend was always pushing me to do things which were two or three steps further than I really felt comfortable doing. My friend had me doing silly things that kids like to do—and think are clever. We would go and ring people's door bells, and then we would run around the back of the house so that no one was there when the door was opened. We would make crank calls on the phone: "Hello, is your refrigerator running? Yes, well you better go catch it." Hilarious, I know. We also used to ride our bikes to the big grocery store nearby and spend half the day floating around and filling up on all the food samples. We'd eat cheese and cookies and little pieces of sausage until someone finally kicked us out.

I always felt bad participating in these acts of little boy naughtiness. I didn't want to seem like a loser to my friend, but I knew the things we were doing were not quite right. I'm sure we've all felt that way before—with big things and small things. We know in our gut that what we're doing is wrong, but push aside the conscience convicting us of evil.

## 2. A SEARED CONSCIENCE

1 Timothy 4:2 speaks of "the insincerity of liars whose consciences are seared." This is going one step further than having an evil conscience. A seared conscience is one that has been cauterized so that it cannot feel anymore. At this stage, we have ignored our conscience too many times and it no longer works properly.

It's like scar tissue. I have a bit of scar on my elbow from my days as a camp counselor. We often played "capture the flag." It did not matter if they were little students; I still wanted to get their flag. I would run to their side of the campground, find their flag, and run back. I took it very seriously, and so did the other boys. One particular occasion, I was running back to the safe side of the camp when one of the students, trying to tag me from behind, managed to take a chunk of flesh out of my elbow. There was blood dripping down my arm. I was quite the hero as I continued to play despite such a dramatic injury! I still have a mark to commemorate my heroism. Today that spot on my elbow is nothing but scar tissue. You can poke it and scratch it, and I won't feel a thing.

A better analogy might be frostbite from the cold. In Michigan, we get lots of snow during the winter. The weather can be dreadfully cold for weeks on end. It's important to bundle up from head to toe. If you go outside without your gloves on, your hands will get cold and start to hurt. That's bad. What's worse is when they stop hurting. If you are outside long enough, the pain actually starts to go away. This is when you are really in danger, as nerve endings get damaged and frostbite sets in. Stay out long enough and you are at real risk of suffering permanent damage, perhaps even losing some of your fingers.

The same thing happens in the Christian life. We can develop spiritual frostbite. When we first do something we know we should not, we feel that twinge of conscience. We feel pain in our extremities like we do when we are outside in the cold. Yet if we persist in doing what is foolish, there comes a time when we start to feel better about engaging in such behavior. We no longer consider that it is wrong. The bad stuff doesn't feel so bad anymore, which is when we are in great spiritual peril. This is the danger of having a seared conscience.

## 3. A DEFILED CONSCIENCE

The next category is a defiled conscience, which we see in Titus 1:15: "To the pure, all things are pure, but to the defiled and unbelieving, nothing is pure; but both their minds and their consciences are defiled." A defiled conscience is one that is completely out of whack. It celebrates what is impure and denigrates what is good.

Think of the university student whose conscience is so scrambled that he or she *does not* feel guilty to go out and get wasted, and to sleep around on a weekend, but who instead *does* feel bad about themselves if they do not go out and party, and experience college life as they think they should.

Even as Christians our conscience can become defiled. We can get all mixed up so that we fear offending others more than we fear offending God. So instead of standing up for a biblical definition of marriage, we feel guilty for insisting that sexual intimacy is reserved for the context of marriage between a man and a woman. Even though the church, in most places around the globe and for 99% of its history, has espoused the same basic principles regarding sex and marriage, we can feel that the revisionist ethic is noble and the Bible's teaching is too embarrassing to mention. This could be evidence of a defiled conscience that now calls evil "good" and good "evil."

## 4. A WEAK CONSCIENCE

So far we have looked at three varieties of a misfiring conscience: an evil conscience, a seared conscience, and a defiled conscience. There is one other type that is a little different. It is a weak conscience, and is mentioned by Paul in 1

Corinthians 8:7: "not all possess this knowledge. But some, through former association with idols, eat food as really offered to an idol, and their conscience, being weak, is defiled." It is a complicated argument that Paul gives here in 1 Corinthians 8 and then again in chapter 10. Here's the gist: instead of having a conscience that allows us to get away with things we should not do, a weak conscience accuses us of things that are not really wrong.

The classic example, which Paul gives in 1 Corinthians 8 and 10, is that of food sacrificed to idols. Think about the difficulties many new Christians were facing in the ancient world. People who had been worshiping idols, including sacrificing food to these idols, for their entire lives were wondering what to do with this food now that they were Christians. Was it safe to eat food sacrificed to idols? Was it no big deal? Or did it mean you were still participating in idolatry in some way to eat the food? I once heard the story of a family in an animistic culture who used to worship a tree in their backyard, but then, after becoming Christians, they began hanging laundry on the tree instead.

The situation may sound humorous to us, but they wrestled with whether it was best to stay away from the tree altogether. What do we do with objects and practices that were once associated with evil and idolatry?

When our conscience tells us not to do something even though we have complete freedom and liberty to do it, that's a weak conscience. This is what Paul has in mind when he talks about "a stumbling block" (1 Cor. 8:9). Most Christians misunderstand this term. We think of a stumbling block as something that offends someone else or tempts someone else to sin. But that's not exactly what Paul has in mind. According to the Apostle Paul, we put up a stumbling block when we encourage others, by our freedom, to do something that is against their conscience.

Take drinking alcohol, for example. There are many Christians who are happy to drink in moderation once they are of age. There are others who grew up hearing that Christians should never drink. Certainly, some people teach that in the United States. I grew up in a conservative church and often thought serious

Christians never touched alcohol. To this day, I am a teetotaler myself, mostly for reasons of health and taste. Yet I now believe that Christians have freedom to enjoy a glass of beer or wine in moderation.

Here is where the issue of alcohol can become a stumbling block if we're not careful. Let's suppose you are sure of your freedom in Christ and have a stout ale from time to time, without any twinge of conscience. One night, your teetotal friend comes over. She tries not to judge you for drinking, but you know she feels very uncomfortable around alcohol and would feel terrible to drink it herself. Knowing that Christians are free to enjoy an alcoholic beverage every once in awhile, you chastise your friend. "Come on, lighten up. Jesus turned water into wine. Let me buy you a drink." This is what Paul means by a stumbling block. The problem is not that you drink and experience freedom in Christ. The conscience should not condemn us for a glass of wine. But when the conscience does accuse us, we should not ignore the conscience. We put a stumbling block in someone else's path when we encourage them to do what they feel is wrong, even if we know that for others it may be right.

The same problem can arise in different scenarios. You may be happy as a Christian to go to the movies. You may think it is acceptable to see a film, even though some of those accompanying you are uncomfortable with the choice. Let's assume the movie doesn't have anything truly objectionable; it is genuinely a matter of conscience. What should you do with your friends who won't see what you feel fine to see? If they are good friends, they won't judge you (again, assuming the content is not obviously lewd). And if you are a good friend, you won't press them to do something their conscience will not allow.

Paul urges us that even when we encounter a weak conscience—even when we are being accused of doing something that is truly not wrong—we need to take heed of it. We may want to inform the other person's conscience and correct their thinking so that they no longer feel bad for doing something acceptable. There is certainly a time for this kind of teaching. But unless they are convinced by the Bible, we should not urge other Christians to violate their consciences. In essence, Paul says, "Don't flaunt your freedom, and don't convince people to go against the conscience. Because when you do, you only reinforce the idea that the conscience should be ignored. And if they get in a habit of ignoring the conscience, they will end up sinning—not just in their heads, but for real and against God." That is what Paul means when he instructs us to "take care that this right of yours does not somehow become a stumbling block to the weak" (1 Cor. 8:9).

Of course, in the long run, the goal is for the weak conscience to be instructed so that it can function properly. Eating food sacrificed to idols was not objectively wrong. The Corinthians should have learned that. The weak conscience is not working the way it should. Our sense of right of wrong must be informed by the Bible, not by cultural taboos or peer pressure.

**5**

# THE WAY TO A CLEAR CONSCIENCE

Our consciences must constantly be probed and changed by the Holy Spirit working through the Word of God. As we have seen, they can be evil, defined, seared or weak, but the goal is to have what the Bible calls a good or a clear conscience. The importance of pursuing a clear conscience is so common in the New Testament that we may have overlooked this critical theme.

Here are a few instances:

*So I always take pains to have a clear conscience toward both God and man (Acts 24:16).*

*The aim of our charge is love that issues from a pure heart and a good conscience and a sincere faith (1 Tim. 1:5).*

*They must hold the mystery of the faith with a clear conscience (1 Tim. 3:9).*

*. . . [have] a good conscience, so that, when you are slandered, those who revile your good behavior in Christ may be put to shame (1 Pet. 3:16).*

Clearly, part of our experience as a Christian ought to be the testimony of a good conscience. But how do we get there? What are the steps we must take to have a clean conscience? Fundamentally, there are only two steps to take.

## 1. TURN FROM SIN

The first step to the blessing of a clear conscience is to turn from sin when our conscience informs us that what we are doing (or about to do, or have done) is wrong.

I fear many of us have gotten adept at shoving aside the conscience. What about the movies we watch? Or the shows we binge on? Or the hours wasted on the internet? Or the way we spend our money? Or the way we treat our parents? Or the language we use? Or the things we laugh at? Do we pay much attention to the conscience anymore?

I think if Christians from an earlier time could come and visit us and our churches, there would be two things that would surprise them most.

First, they would be absolutely amazed by our phenomenal prosperity. We have more comforts and conveniences than kings and queens had for almost all of human history.

Second, I think they would be amazed by how comfortable we have become with sensuality. We might question our entertainment choices, but only briefly. "Oh man, that movie had some bad parts. I almost walked out five times. But I managed to get through it." I am not saying that we have to stay away from watching movies and television and the internet entirely. I have enjoyed all three at different times. But try this: do not watch TV or movies for a month or so, and then when you turn it all back on, see if you notice things you had stopped caring about. I now look back at some movies I watched when I was younger and am disappointed in what I used to think was no big deal.

Maybe it's not entertainment that is the issue for you and your friends. Maybe your conscience pricks you about the jokes you tell or your attitude at work. Maybe there are sins you've kept hidden and have never dealt with. Maybe even now you are a living a double life and hoping no one will see through your charade.

Don't ignore your conscience. Sometimes we see so clearly into someone else's life but not into our own. Are you kicking against the goads? Are your grieving the Holy Spirit? What is your conscience telling you? Is the Holy Spirit pleading with you to see what you have refused to see? When conscience accuses us of wrong, let us turn from the sin with all haste.

## 2. TURN TO CHRIST

But don't stop there. Turn from sin, and turn to Christ. As Christians, we are meant to experience a clean conscience. We see a great picture of this in John Bunyan's book *The*

*Pilgrim's Progress*. Christian journeys with a great weight on his back—the knowledge of his sin and guilt—before finally unloading his burden at the foot of the cross. Like Christian, we are meant to experience this freedom. "If we confess our sins, he [God] is faithful and just to forgive us our sins and to cleanse us from all unrighteousness" (1 John 1:9).

I wonder whether you have ever noticed those words "he is faithful and just." We would expect it to say, "he is faithful and *merciful*," or "he is faithful and *loving*." Yet it says, "he is faithful and *just*." God's mercy for sinners is also an act of justice, because Christ has fully paid for all our debts. God doesn't say, "Your sins are no big deal. Never mind." He says, "Your sins deserve an infinite punishment, but that punishment has been met by my Son."

In Christ, it is possible to live with a clean conscience. Hebrews 9:9 speaks of the "gifts and sacrifices" offered under the Old Testament regulations—offerings that could not "perfect the conscience of the worshiper." By contrast, Hebrews 10:22 declares that through the blood of Jesus Christ our hearts can be "sprinkled clean from an evil conscience and our bodies washed with pure water." This is why we must turn from sin and to Christ.

## LIVING THE LIFE WE WERE MEANT TO LIVE

As Christians, we are both too hard and too easy on ourselves. In one sense, we are too hard because we are susceptible to the danger of introspection. Some reading this book, just by your upbringing or by your temperament, will be tempted to analyze yourself to death (maybe literally). I have a very good friend, a dear brother to whom I look up, who is this way inclined. When we were reading a book by one of the Puritans, he said, "Kevin, whenever I read the Puritans, I feel like I am not Christian." My friend has good theology, but he also has such a tender conscience and is so prone to introspection that he can easily feel helpless and hopeless. On another occasion, when I preached a few years ago from 1 John, he said, "Kevin, when you talk about holiness, would you remember that there are people like me in the congregation who are too aware of our sin; we need to know that there is a Savior."

Gloomy self-absorption is bad for us (and bad Puritanism to boot!). Do not think that being a serious Christian means undertaking morbid introspection, with the mentality that says, "If I am really spiritual, I will constantly look at myself and feel terrible." We can be too hard on ourselves when we think we are not doing well unless we constantly feel bad.

The other danger is when we are too easy on ourselves, quickly ignoring and suppressing our conscience. We get used to living with feelings of low-level guilt and failure. I think this is the experience of most Christians. The Bible says our goal is to have a clean conscience, which means when we are right to feel guilty about our sin, we are to run quickly to the cross. Yet so often that is not what we do. We are to say, "Lord, forgive me. I took a second look again. I was angry with my children again. I was so impatient. Forgive me." Then we will know God's favor as our heavenly Father. We are not meant to live with a low-level, persistent sense of guilt and shame. We are meant, as the Lord Jesus taught us, to daily confess our sins and know his favor.

1 Corinthians 4:3-4 is an absolutely astounding passage in helping us to understand this. I think it is one of the most life-altering passages if we really can appropriate it. Paul says, "it is a very small thing that I should be judged by you or by any human court. In fact, I do not even judge myself. I am not aware of anything against myself, but I am not thereby acquitted. It is the Lord who judges me."

Our initial reaction to this passage is probably to question what planet Paul is living on. He is not aware of anything? He is not accountable? Paul does not mean that he has not sinned. Elsewhere he describes himself as the chief of sinners (1 Tim. 1:15). Nor does he mean that he is perfectly sanctified. In Romans 7 he talks about the wrestling of a Christian against sin, and this being his own experience. He does not even say that if his conscience is fine, everything must be good. He admits, "I am not thereby acquitted. It is the Lord who judges me."

But don't miss Paul's astounding confidence. He says in effect, "I could be wrong about this, but as far as I can tell, I am walking with the Lord." He's not perfect. But he is forgiven. When his conscience accuses him, he goes to the cross and finds forgiveness. You get the sense Paul is not living a defeated Christian life, moping around feeling a low-level sense that "I'm a failure; I'm terrible; God's angry at me." Paul lives his days in freedom with a good conscience. He turns; he repents; he confesses; he receives forgiveness; and then he enjoys this wonderful relationship with his heavenly Father. Paul is not claiming to be infallible in self-examination, but what he says is remarkable.

I think most Christians have very little experience with this kind of Christian existence. We go from morbidity, to introspection, to moments of victory, to feelings of failure again. Of course, we fight and wrestle. And yet, this is not the same as constant gloom and doom. We ought to put our head on our pillow at night knowing we have been forgiven, we have a heavenly Father who loves us, and we can have a clean conscience. Mothers, who are wired for comparison all the time, find this especially hard. They are too quick to conclude, "What a terrible mother I am. I must not be doing a good job with my kids—I'm sure they aren't doing as well as they should. And I'm sure my house is so much messier than everyone else's." An older mom once gave me these wise words: "Kevin, most parents think their children are either the best children—the brightest, most special children in the whole world—or that they are the worst failure of a child. Both of those parents are wrong." That was a good observation.

If we walk around feeling all the time like we are a failure as a Christian, a failure as a parent, and a failure as a pastor, we have not grasped the gift of the gospel. This is not what it means to have the ministry of the Holy Spirit in our life.

How wonderful it is when we turn from self and sin, and turn to Christ and Christlikeness, when we can be clean, forgiven, and free. Of all the times you've given your testimony, have you ever testified to the great gift of having a clean conscience? The Puritans used to say that the conscience is either the greatest friend or the greatest enemy in the world. Just remember: it's supposed to be the Christian's friend.

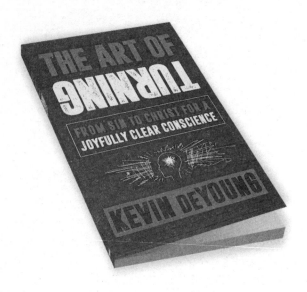

**10Publishing** is the publishing house of **10ofThose**.
It is committed to producing quality Christian
resources that are biblical and accessible.

**www.10ofthose.com** is our online retail arm selling
thousands of quality books at discounted prices.

For information contact: **info@10ofthose.com**
or check out our website: **www.10ofthose.com**